Wisdom
AND
Wealth

7 ANCIENT SECRETS
OF KING SOLOMON

BY DON JACOBS

Dedication

I learned some of life's greatest lessons from my parents, Don & Darlene. Thank you for teaching me love, hard work, honesty and faith through your living example.

God has given me the greatest blessing a man could ask for...Terry, my wife, friend and walking partner. Thank you for your love and ongoing encouragement for over 25 years.

Stephen, my Wednesday lunch partner for over seven years. I can't thank you enough for your input, constant support and believing in me. I think I owe you lunch.

Catherine, I greatly appreciate your help in editing and designing this book. You have helped me turn one of my dreams into a reality.

Preface

Solomon, whose name means peace and
prosperity, has always been considered the wisest of
the wise and richest of the rich. About 970 B.C.,
Solomon became King of Israel and reigned for forty
years. Although he built an empire of incredible
military strength, amassed wealth that can only be
imagined, and built the legendary Temple of
Jerusalem, Solomon became most famous through
the ages for his wisdom.

Soon after he became king, Solomon went to the
shrine at Gibeon to pray. When God appeared to him
in a dream and asked him to name whatever blessing
he most desired, Solomon answered, "The **wisdom**
to be a good judge and ruler to my people." Pleased
with this reply, God bestowed upon Solomon not
only **wisdom,** but also **wealth, power** and **victory**
over his enemies.

Solomon is credited as the author of a remarkable
work of practical philosophy in the book of Proverbs
and of lyrical poetry in the *Song of Solomon*. History
records that Solomon also assembled a mighty
commercial empire, stretching to every corner of the
known world. Each year, Solomon received **25 tons
of gold**, about $308 million by today's reckoning, in
addition to countless jewels and other gifts. By
marrying the sisters and daughters of other kings, he
strengthened his political position and created
alliances that led to an unprecedented era of peace
and prosperity for his kingdom.

This prosperity was the cornerstone of Solomon's
passion for building. His construction program,
which included the royal palace and the mighty

Temple of Jerusalem, were unmatched in splendor. Eventually, Solomon's palace is said to have housed 700 wives and 300 concubines, with servants and military staff as well.

After a few decades, the prosperity of Israel began to dwindle. The increases in wealth amassed by Solomon lead to increases in extravagance. Solomon's unlimited power and political strength led to pride and self-indulgence. The lavish spending on royal construction projects led to a revolt against high taxes and the system of forced labor required to build the palaces and royal residences.

Solomon, the wisest of the wise and richest of the rich, eventually failed to heed his own philosophy of wisdom, kindness and good judgment. He fell prey to the devouring evils of pride and extravagance, and completely failed to consider his people.

We can learn much from Solomon. His wisdom and the principles set down in **Proverbs** teach us, but so does his decline. We can take the best of Solomon's story, listen and live by the code of Solomon, and choose **not** to fall into the traps set for us by wealth and power.

Using quotations from the Book of Proverbs translated in the King James, Revised Standard and Good News® editions of the Bible, this guide brings together keys to the wisdom and wealth of Solomon. Use them, and remember Solomon's story.

Don Jacobs

Introduction:

Here are the Proverbs that will help you recognize wisdom and good advice, and understand sayings with deep meaning. They can teach you how to live intelligently and how to be honest, just, and fair. They can make an inexperienced person clever and teach young people how to be resourceful. These Proverbs can even add to the knowledge of the wise and give guidance to the educated...
Proverbs 1:2-6

The complexities of modern life make us all long for a simple set of rules which will allow us to achieve happiness and success. Success is a subjective term, different for every person, but we each want to enjoy life and still have the material possessions we need to give ourselves and our families comfort.

While literally thousands of books are written each year to provide the "self help" many people are looking for, the wisdom and guidance we need to achieve success in today's world are already contained in a book so ancient, it is often overlooked —the book of Proverbs in the Bible.

The wisdom of Solomon is an established fact to nearly everyone. We all know, from our childhood, that Solomon was one of the truly wise, a man who understood much and had wealth beyond measure, power over an entire people and a legacy of respect and honor that carries down to this day.

Wouldn't you be excited by the prospect of Solomon talking directly to you? The fact is, we have Solomon's wisdom, his advice for modern living, and his counsel to guide us toward success. The book of Proverbs **is Solomon's "self help" book,** available to us as it has been to countless generations who have used his secrets to forge a better life for themselves and their families.

Wisdom & Wealth looks at the critical proverbs of Solomon, and applies them to life in any century—even in the new millennium. You will be reminded of many of the things your parents and grandparents tried to teach you, just as Solomon was presenting a guidebook to his offspring. You will be astounded by the way these ancient lessons give us a blueprint for happiness and success today.

THE FIRST SECRET:

Learn to think positively and gain wisdom.

Be careful how you think;
your life is shaped by your thoughts.
Proverbs 4:23

We never stop thinking. We even think while we're asleep. Thoughts race through our brains faster than the speed of light. But we **can** control those thoughts. We can think about good things and not bad, about positive ideas and not negative. In fact, as Solomon points out, we shape our lives by the thoughts we think.

We shape our day, our jobs, our relationships and our feelings about ourselves by our thoughts. We must take care how we think. Think positively about every aspect of your life and shape your life for success.

When you get up in the morning, think about what you are going to do to make this day a great day for you and those around you. Visualize the positive elements of your life and think about each of the good things you enjoy about your life. When speaking to others, focus on the positive aspects of the situation, and try to lead the conversation into positive paths.

*Anyone who thinks and speaks evil
can expect to find nothing good—
only disaster.*
Proverbs 17:20

If you pour dirty water into a clear glass that's what you'll have to drink....dirty water. Your mind is that clear glass—fill it with good thoughts and good words and that's what you will have to draw from all the time.

We all know someone whose major contribution to any conversation is to criticize someone else, complain about the coffee, point out the faults of the government and generally give us a forecast for doom. That kind of person will not achieve success, only disaster. For one thing, disaster is all that person can think about—it fills his mind, and prevents him from moving toward success.

A person who thinks she has the worst job in the world will eventually **have** the worst job in the world—a dead-end position with no advancement, no reward, no positive reinforcement. A spouse who feels trapped in an awful marriage will soon poison the relationship and make that vision a reality. And an individual who constantly doubts his own abilities will never achieve what he is capable of because he will be sunk in a well of despair.

If you think good thoughts and only speak well of others, you can expect good to happen, and success to follow.

Listen, my son,
be wise
and give serious thought
to the way you live.
Proverbs 23:19

Plan your life to get what you want and set goals. Give careful thought to current habits and friendships that may hinder you from achieving the kind of life you're looking for.

Look at a road map of the United States. There are many different roads to take, some going to places you may want to go and others to places you don't. In life we have the ability to choose the roads to the destinations that we call happiness. Right now choose the road of happiness you want and be very specific about what you want from your life. A good family, friends, faith and future success will make you happy.

Hardly anyone is completely satisfied with where he or she is at this particular moment in life. Solomon recommends **being wise** and giving **serious thought** to the way we live. We can do that first of all by listening, by being sensitive to the wisdom around us, and by thinking positively about the way we **want** to live. Then we can follow through and achieve success. But success demands a plan and a plan demands thinking ahead, thinking positively and following the wisdom of Solomon.

Do yourself a favor and learn all you can; then remember what you learn and you will prosper.
Proverbs 19:8

We go to school, we listen to stories from our parents and grandparents, we exchange ideas with our friends. All of this is learning, gaining wisdom. Solomon points out the necessity for continuing to learn all we can throughout life.

In addition, we must **remember** what we learn. The lessons of life, like the lessons of education, stick with us best when we apply them, or use them, in our daily activities. If we don't learn our lessons, we don't move forward, but get stuck in an endless cycle of repeating our mistakes. We prosper by learning and remembering.

Unfortunately, many people today think that school provides the education that is most important for being successful. School is important, but there are far greater lessons to be learned from people who have learned through living, through fortune and bankruptcy, through happiness and depression. These lessons of wisdom are usually free, and can save you time, money and unhappiness.

Truth, wisdom,
learning and good sense—
these are worth paying for,
but are too valuable for you to sell.
Proverbs 23:23

We live in a world that specializes in buying and selling. Sometimes it seems that there is nothing that is not for sale in our society. We are bombarded, day and night, by exhortations to buy, buy, buy. Often the things we are asked to buy promise us nothing except a momentary thrill or a passing entertainment.

Some of the things we can buy promise more tangible rewards: books, music, works of art that can transform the way we look at the world. These things often become our most precious possessions. We buy them, and will not sell them. And those precious touchstones can bring us wisdom.

But some wisdom and learning comes to us the hard way: through suffering, through joy, through experiencing life. This is the best and most lasting way to pay for truth. And when we buy wisdom, learning and good sense through our very humanness, that truth becomes a part of us—not to be given up, at any price.

Happy is the man who becomes wise,
who comes to have understanding.
There is more profit in it
than there is in silver;
it is worth more to you than gold.
Proverbs 3:13

Wisdom allows you to make decisions in every aspect of your life without worry, hesitation or regrets. When we are free of the worry and fear which often accompany the decisions we make in our personal or business life, we are always happier. We have a better outlook on life and other people. This is why true wisdom is worth more to you than gold, because gold cannot buy such worry-free happiness. Can you put a value on total happiness? Most people would give everything for it. With wisdom, it's free.

Understanding is the knowledge of people and circumstances that sets us apart. Those who don't care enough to try to understand are selfish and end up unhappy. But those of us who keep learning, keep growing and keep adding to our store of wisdom will be happy—and will be more successful in life. Wisdom is a **precious commodity** and the foundation of success.

Teach a child how he should live
and he will remember it all his life.
Proverbs 22:6

The question so many of us ask is: "How do I teach my child how he should live?" And, of course, there is no easy answer. But there is no denying the wisdom and truth of this proverb. Children, instructed correctly, will remember the lessons of childhood and have a happier life when they become older. That is the very foundation of parenthood.

But we are charged with the task of knowing how our children—and we—should live, so that we may teach them. We want to teach our children the right way, the Way which is Right. The Right Way contains the simple concepts of right and wrong in which all of us are grounded: the Ten Commandments, the Golden Rule and the courtesy which makes society work. Isn't it true that children trained in those principles will find it easier, throughout life, to stay on the path that leads to happiness and success? And **that** is the way all of us should live, after all.

Wisdom offers you long life
as well as wealth and honor.
Wisdom can make your life pleasant
and lead you safely through it.
Those who become wise are happy;
wisdom will give them life.
Proverbs 3:16-18

When we learn to live well, we learn to live long. Modern medicine agrees that a life with more happiness and less stress will be a long life. We are finding more and more that the simple fact of being happy adds years to our life expectancy, just as things that make us happy, from laughing at jokes to playing with children, make us feel better every day.

Knowing this, and knowing how to make ourselves and others happy is a form of wisdom that doesn't have to just come from age. Similarly, when we acquire the wisdom that comes from thinking good thoughts and learning more about ourselves and others, we acquire wealth and honor. Just as Solomon received wisdom as a gift from God, we can aspire to that wisdom ourselves. Wisdom adds great value to our lives.

*Keep company with the wise
and you will become wise.
If you make friends with
stupid people,
you will be ruined.*
Proverbs 13:20

"You can't soar with the eagles if you run with the turkeys," claims an old saying. Solomon understood that not only do we define ourselves by our companions, but we establish goals for ourselves according to the company we keep. If we associate with those who want to keep learning and growing as people, we will add to our own wisdom. If we don't, we won't achieve the personal success we strive for.

You may find wise people among your friends, co-workers, neighbors or business associates. Anyone you can learn something from can be considered "wise." Make a list of those people you **know** you can learn from. There is wisdom to be gained from every friendship, meeting and interaction between people. Seek the wisdom in others.

How to start thinking positively

1. **Fill your brain with good thoughts.**

2. **Turn _every_ conversation into a conversation with positives.**

3. **Set the goals you want to achieve for happiness.**
   A. Family
   B. Success
   C. Relationships

How to gain wisdom

1. Make a list of the people you think are wise and associate with <u>them</u>.

2. Read books that provide you with new insights and knowledge.

3. Make a list of areas in which you want to gain wisdom.

THE SECOND SECRET:

**Self-confidence and hard work
will help you achieve your goals.**

*Look straight ahead
with honest confidence;
don't hang your head in shame.*
Proverbs 4:25

Confidence is "assurance of one's own ability." Your confidence will color every aspect of your life, from business to personal relationships. Unfortunately, confidence is often a delicate balance between assurance and unawareness of our own limitations. The criticism of others can unduly affect our confidence, too.

But Solomon's words give us the balance point we need. Look straight ahead, face life with a confident smile and posture—don't hang your head. If you receive criticism, try to determine if it is hidden wisdom and will really make you a better person. If so, take it to heart. If not, ignore it and keep looking "straight ahead in confidence!"

Being cheerful keeps you healthy.
It is slow death
to be gloomy all the time.
Proverbs 17:22

Cheerfulness and confidence go hand-in-hand. If you are confident, you naturally feel better and are more cheerful. People who lack self-confidence have a negative outlook but can't make the connection between that negative outlook and the gloom around them.

If you can't immediately be confident, start by being cheerful every day. This will bring out the best in people around you and increase your confidence, which will increase your cheerfulness. Next time you see a baby or a young child, give them a big smile and watch the reaction. Adults respond that way, too. Find something to be cheerful about every day—it will build your confidence and your success factor in every endeavor!

Your will to live
can sustain you when you are sick,
but if you lose it,
your last hope is gone.
Proverbs 18:14

What is your will to live but **confidence** in yourself and your future? People who lose their will to live but don't actually die often live their lives as if disappointed they did **not** die. If you lose confidence in yourself and those around you, you lose hope— the lifeline that ties us to a happy future.

How strong is your will to live? It should be unbreakable. If you sometimes feel it weakening, you need to exercise your self confidence, just as you exercise a weak muscle. **Focus** on the positive things in your life; **visualize** the future and what you want in life, so you have a dream to live for, and **project** cheerfulness and self-confidence to all around you.

*Enthusiasm without knowledge
is not good;
impatience will get you into trouble.*
Proverbs 19:2

"Fools rush in where angels fear to tread."
Enthusiasm is a powerful force for good, and closely
tied to a strong self-confidence. But we are taught
here that we can easily get in over our heads if we
don't temper that enthusiasm with knowledge.

Imagine that you've always wanted to start a
restaurant because of your love of cooking. Your self-
confidence and enthusiasm for the project may carry
you successfully through to your goal. However,
your chances of success are much greater if you add
some business and management knowledge to the
mix. A lack of knowledge can create situations which
are destructive to self-confidence and enthusiasm.

*No matter how much
a lazy person may want something,
he will never get it.
A hard worker
will get everything he wants.*
Proverbs 13:4

Talk to the people you think are successful. The vast majority of them will tell you that their success is built on hard work. Henry Ford said "The harder I work, the luckier I get." and Thomas Edison is credited with saying that "Genius is one percent inspiration and 99 percent perspiration."

Luck doesn't follow hard-working people, success does. Others seek out hard-working people when problems need solutions—and that's where opportunity lies. The best way to achieve the goals you seek—strong, healthy relationships, success in business, good health, peace of mind—is to direct your best efforts toward those goals. You may not reach all your goals but you will accomplish a great deal more through consistent hard work than through lazy indifference.

Show me a man who does a good job,
and I will show you a man
who is better than most
and worthy of the company of kings.
Proverbs 22:29

We have come to under-appreciate "a good job." Too often, we settle for "good enough," instead of a good job. The person who works to do his best at the task at hand is rare, and thus will be singled out from among others who are unwilling to do their best.

Those people who do a good job and do it better than it has been done before are recognized and rewarded for their work. Too few people see the long term benefits of doing a job better than is expected. Once you've raised your standards of performance, others will notice and both your reputation and compensation will grow.

...a lazy man will never have money,
but an aggressive man will get rich.
Proverbs 11:16

It's almost too obvious, but lazy people just don't seem to get ahead. When is the last time you saw a want ad for "experienced, honest lazy production workers." Lazy people are easily singled out in a workforce and never receive the advancements that hard working people do.

Further, Solomon tells us that "an aggressive man will get rich." Being aggressive means being willing to do a little more than the next guy, or tackling a job that nobody else wants to do. Success follows those who are willing to extend themselves and be aggressive.

The more easily you get your wealth,
the sooner you will lose it.
The harder it is to earn,
the more you will have.
Proverbs 13:11

Have you ever dreamed of winning the lottery or inheriting millions? Most of us have. But many people who have obtained wealth quickly have not only lost it all, but found no happiness in their sudden wealth. The unique problems that come with such wealth can be worse than the ones you faced before.

On the other hand, when you earn your money, and learn the value of each dollar you earn, you can grow in the wisdom of handling your money. The false sense of power and security that comes with sudden wealth can't compare with the patient gains of earning and investing wisely.

How to increase your self-confidence

1. Talk to yourself, reminding yourself, "I'm really good at..."

2. Associate with people who make you feel good about yourself.

3. Face the world with a positive, cheerful outlook every day.

Improving your work habits

1. Be willing to go the "extra mile." List the things you can do to set yourself apart.

2. Utilize your time wisely and efficiently. List three ways to improve your time management skills.

3. Delegate responsibilities that others can do, leaving you the time to the things that actually require your effort.

THE THIRD SECRET:

Honesty is one of the keys to happiness and long life.

Never say anything that isn't true.
Have nothing to do with lies
and misleading words.
Proverbs 4:24

It's easy to stretch the truth. Sometimes we can even justify a small white lie to keep from hurting someone. The problem with any lie is that someone always discovers the truth, forcing us to tell another lie to cover up, or telling the truth in the end. Better to tell the truth up front and avoid the confusion and embarrassment of being caught in a lie.

People do business with people they trust. Friendship is based on honesty and trust. We all know that the best way to be trustworthy is to always tell the truth. It sounds so simple, but is so often overlooked in favor of cultivating a "good image." Let your image be that of an honest person who can always be trusted. Tell the truth and people will respect you for it.

*Be kind and honest
and you will live a long life;
others will respect you
and treat you fairly.*
Proverbs 21:21

Since so many of us are influenced by the way others see us and treat us, it should be simple to follow this wise advice. When you are kind and honest, others will respond to you in the same way and your life will be better in so many ways. If you are dishonest, others will hear of it, and your reputation will be tarnished and your life will be diminished by the ill will of others. Dishonesty doesn't stay a secret very long.

But how does honesty increase our life expectancy? The answer is stress, that great source of illness, despair and negative emotions. Kindness and honesty are the keys to simple, daily lack of stress. Think about it: if you didn't have anger, deception and anxiety in your life, wouldn't you be healthier, happier and more likely to have a long, productive, successful life? Being treated fairly and respected by others is a good way to live.

*Better to be poor and honest
than rich and dishonest.*
Proverbs 28:6

44

"How rich and dishonest?" some people would ask. But getting ahead through dishonesty is **not** a recipe for lasting success. A "quick score" at the expense of others will not earn you friends, or business associates who put their trust in you.

How much is your good name worth in the long haul? Would you sacrifice any future credibility for dishonest financial gain? Better to trust in your abilities to work hard and follow up honest opportunities.

People who promise things
that they never give
are like clouds and wind
that bring no rain.
Proverbs 25:14

No one can afford to be just rumbling thunder and clouds that sail over without delivering the life-giving rain. We must live up to our promises to maintain our relationships, with friends, with family, with business associates. Broken promises force people to label you as undependable and dishonest, undermining your friendships and business.

Once you've been dishonest, you not only make it easy for yourself to continue a practice of dishonesty, you also set the stage for people to despise you for your dishonesty. A reputation as an honest person is one of the hardest things to regain, once it has been lost. Why jeopardize it in the first place?

Being honest

1. Close your eyes and remember the last time you told a lie. Was it really necessary? What could you have done to avoid lying?

2. Be fair in all your dealings with other people.

3. Evaluate your integrity. Think of a recent conversation in which you were dishonest. How you could you have changed events by being honest instead?

THE FOURTH SECRET:

Modesty will earn you respect and praise.

Arrogance will bring your downfall,
but if you are humble,
you will be respected.
Proverbs 29:23

Modesty is not easy when everything in your life is going well and it seems you're unbeatable. However, it's just that time which calls most for being modest. We all have a tendency to boast a little, if only to let others know just how well we are doing.

If we can restrain that impulse, and be modest when there seems little reason for humility, we illustrate a strength of character that most people just don't have. That will earn the respect of others, and makes for closer friendships and business relationships. Arrogance **always** drives people away and reveals immaturity and a weak personality.

*Conceited people
do not like to be corrected;
they never ask for advice
from those who are wiser.*
Proverbs 15:12

Strange that the people who need advice most often are the people who listen least. Conceited people do not welcome the help of others who may be able to point out their weaknesses and make them better people.

It's a good idea to ask others for their opinion, rather than assuming that you are always right. Such conceit makes for tough times when you actually need help, and the people who can give it only remember an earlier arrogance.

*Never boast about tomorrow.
You don't know what will happen
between now and then.*
Proverbs 27:1

Just when we think we are in control and nothing can stop us, something goes wrong. It does no good to boast about how well we're doing or where we'll be in the future. Things change too fast to predict what's going to happen.

People who boast about their accomplishments or gains usually have a big cheering section when things fall apart. Save your boasts for the successes of others and it then becomes praise.

Let other people praise you,
even strangers;
never do it yourself.
Proverbs 27:2

The praise of others is the biggest confidence builder of all. But praising yourself does not have the same effect. When others praise you, you feel great about life and about other people. You even feel like giving some praise back.

When you praise others, you make their day and you start a chain of positive energy that will come back to you. You don't have to be close friends or office pals with someone to give praise. When you observe something being done well, or done right, praise that person for his effort, even if he or she is a stranger. You'll be surprised how quickly that positive feeling returns to make **you** feel good.

People who are proud
will soon be disgraced.
It is wiser to be modest.
Proverbs 11:2

Pride can blind a person to truth and reality. We all have some pride, but we need to recognize when our pride controls us and leads us to ruin. Our pride can be the very source of our disgrace. We must recognize that we are not in control of things. When that fact catches up with someone who thinks he or she has it all, there's a long freefall back down to reality.

Someone who is boasting comes across as needing recognition or a pat on the back—a clear case of insecurity on display. Some boasting is an attempt to make others feel inferior—an ugly way to deal with anyone. People respect those who do well and are modest about their achievements. Feeling pride is one thing—shouting about your accomplishments is quite another!

Achieving modesty

1. Compliment or praise three people today, even if they are strangers. Everyone appreciates recognition.

2. Compliment yourself often for jobs well done, but never boast to others.

3. List two people who you admire that are modest. Spend time with them and learn from them.

THE FIFTH SECRET:

If you learn to listen to others
and control your anger,
others will listen to you.

You will have to live with the consequences of everything you say.
Proverbs 18:20

If everyone believed they would have to live with the consequences of all their words, think of how much more careful we would be about blurting things out! The fact is, our words are **our word**. That is, what we say becomes our promise and our belief. Don't say anything you are not willing to live with forever.

"What goes around, comes around" is a saying most of us have heard. Though often used in reference to things we **do**, it is also true of things we **say**. If you don't want something you say to come back to haunt you, it's best not said at all.

If one gives answer before hearing,
it is folly and shame.
Proverbs 18:20

One of the most misunderstood and under-utilized elements of good communication is **listening**. How can we exchange ideas and share wisdom if we don't listen? Too many of us are preparing our answer before we hear the question. And in a world that seems overly filled with snappy comebacks and sarcastic jabs, listening carefully and speaking at the appropriate time is becoming a lost art.

Don't fall into the trap of talking without listening, or speaking without hearing. The wisest man is often the one who speaks the least and listens the most—and he's the one who is absorbing the most knowledge, too. Be a good communicator by becoming a good listener.

*Thoughtless words can wound
as deeply as any sword,
but wisely spoken words can heal.*
Proverbs 12:18

Thoughtless words are those spoken without wisdom. Remember the popular saying "Engage brain before opening mouth?" Don't speak without thinking, or you may wound someone instead of speaking healing words.

We have the power to hurt or heal people with our words. Knowing that the right words can help people, we should choose those words very carefully. Think of yourself as a doctor, and the medicines you have to heal and help people are your words.

A gossip can never keep a secret.
Stay away from people
who talk too much.
Proverbs 20:19

How many babblers do you know? These people are simply talking all the time—and often about things they shouldn't be telling. Those who collect gossip do so for one purpose—to tell others at their earliest possible opportunity! Sometimes it's fun to learn these juicy little tidbits about other people. But do you want the babblers of the world to be talking about you?

Gossip cannot be divided into good and bad, friendly and malicious, as we so often try to do. Gossip—the sharing of secret or negative information about someone not present to defend himself—is always bad, always destructive and always, in the end, makes the gossiper look bad. Don't reveal secrets, and don't associate with those who do. Life is too short to wallow in the mud of gossip.

Worry can rob you of happiness,
but kind words will cheer you up.
Proverbs 12:25

We have learned that we get kind words back by giving them to others. When we are worried about something, we **need** to hear something positive from others to ease our anxiety. This tells us that we also need to be there when others are worrying, to give them kind words to cheer them.

Simply remember that everyone needs a kind word from time to time. A kind word can turn someone's bad day into a great day. Think of the power you have—to help your family, friends and co-workers feel good.

*There is more hope for a stupid fool
than for someone
who speaks without thinking.*
Proverbs 29:20

Ever notice how children will often blurt out something embarrassing with no thought as to the consequences of their words? What is a humorous honesty in children can be something more serious for adults. People who do not think before speaking can really put their feet in their mouth. A fool has the excuse of not knowing better. A child is unaware of the full meaning of many of his words. But as responsible adults, trained and eager to learn wisdom, we have no excuse.

Part of the process of thinking before speaking is **listening** and understanding the words and feelings of those who are around us. We weigh the meaning of the words we have heard, we attempt to gauge the personalities of the people we are with. We are sensitive to the situation. We utilize all that we have learned about people and language before speaking. This way, we find the right road to success and happiness.

*Kind words bring life,
but cruel words crush your spirit.*
Proverbs 15:4

Like a gentle rain followed by warm sunshine, kind words give our spirits what they need to grow. We are lifted up and transformed by friendly, caring words. Similarly, harsh, angry, cruel words diminish us, and take the joy out of life. We actually hurt and the world is a dismal place.

Consider the words you normally use in your conversations with others. Does your vocabulary include really important words that lift people up? Some of these words are: *you, nice, love, great, wonderful, I'm sorry, appreciate* and *thank you*.

Getting involved in an argument
that is none of your business
is like going down the street
and grabbing a dog by the ears.
Proverbs 26:17

Most of us don't go out of our way to look for trouble. We are not likely to pull the ears of a strange dog, nor do we dodge traffic on a busy street for fun. But how many times do people jump into the middle of an argument? Sometimes, it is for the best possible reason—to try to help achieve a resolution, or stop two friends from disagreeing. But how often is such a course of action successful?

A wise person realizes that the interference of a third party more often leads to further misunderstanding. Indeed, the third person can become the target for both quarreling parties. Getting in the middle of something that doesn't concern you can be dangerous—as dangerous as dealing with that dog in the street. If you feel you must intervene, talk to one of the arguing parties privately, and simply express your concern.

If you cannot control your anger,
you are as helpless
as a city without walls,
open to attack.
Proverbs 25:28

When you are angry, you are simply not operating with all your faculties. Your brain is fuzzy with emotion, your respiration is shallow and speeded up, and your heart is pumping wildly. You are incapable of thinking clearly or doing your best at anything. You are vulnerable.

We need to remember that anger has a negative effect on us emotionally and physically. The combination of loss of control emotionally and physically can destroy us without the help of anyone else. You can only alter the negative effects of anger by controlling it.

Don't make friends with people who have hot, violent tempers. You might learn their habits and not be able to change.
Proverbs 22:24-25

It's hard to keep your head when all around you people are losing theirs, to paraphrase the old poem. It's even harder if you spend all your time with people who easily lose their tempers. Once again, it's a case of associating with the kind of people you want to be like, instead of making friends with those whose bad habits you can't help but pick up.

Those people with low flashpoints are not only sapping their own levels of health, happiness and success, they are also poisoning the atmosphere around them with negative feelings and unnecessary scenes. Learn not to be a person who flies off the handle, and stay away from people whose only contribution to any conversation seems to be an angry word.

People with a hot temper
do foolish things;
wiser people remain calm.
Proverbs 14:17

When you are angry, you say and do things you regret later. When we let our emotions take over our more logical side, we end up more often than not admitting, "That was a stupid thing to do." It's something that has happened to all of us.

We learn, as we become older and wiser, to stop, count ten, think and remain calm. No matter how angry or upset you are, stop and think of the long term effects of your actions. If the end result is **not positive**, it's the wrong thing to do. It's that simple.

*Stupid people express
their anger openly,
but sensible people are patient
and hold it back.*
Proverbs 29:11

Everyone feels anger at some time or another. We can't escape the realities of life to the extent of **never** getting angry. But while a foolish person lets his anger carry him away, ranting and raving, the wise person controls his anger and allows it to dissipate harmlessly and quietly.

Displaying our anger with zest only shows our lack of control, logic and discipline. No matter how difficult it may be, never let your anger show. When you've learned to control your anger as easily as you control your words, you'll find it easier to think and discover solutions to the problems at hand. Anger always blinds our logic and problem-solving skills.

Becoming a better communicator

1. Don't let your emotions speak for you. Think before you speak.

2. List the words which make you feel good about yourself. Think about how often you use them with others.

3. Make a list of three people you know who are good listeners. What skills do they show in conversation which make them good communicators?

4. Never communicate with someone when one of you is angry. Give yourself some time to think things through.

THE SIXTH SECRET:

Learn from your mistakes
and appreciate the experience
of others.

Sometimes it takes a painful experience to make us change our ways.
Proverbs 20:30

We learn from our mistakes. We don't have to make mistakes to learn, but it seems that the only way we can break bad habits or change the elements of our personalities which really need changing is by some traumatic or painful experience. It would be better to think things out wisely and come to the right decision, but if we have a painful experience, we must be sure to learn from it.

We all have to go through some tough situations to learn to change. You can lessen the number of those painful experiences by watching others and learning from their mistakes, too. Life is about learning, not being perfect. Don't be afraid to make your mistakes—but try to make them just once and learn from them.

Indulging in luxuries,
wine and rich food
will not make you wealthy.
Proverbs 21:17

We all want nice things, and pleasure is greatly more desirable than pain. But living your life in pursuit of pleasure guarantees that you will not take the time to learn and grow and become the person you want to be. The basics of life—friendship, compassion, wisdom and others—will be passed by in exchange for the pleasures of the moment. It's the classic story of the grasshopper and the ant: the grasshopper pursued the pleasures of life during the summertime, playing while the ant toiled. When winter came, the ant was prepared, while the grasshopper suffered.

Being rich means more than having enough money. Success in life is more than just financial success. But when we love luxury and fast living more than our families or ourselves, we end up more than just poor in our bank accounts. Live simply, and you will live well. Live for others, and you will find more pleasure than you can imagine.

*An intelligent person learns more
from one rebuke
than a fool learns
from being beaten a hundred times.*
Proverbs 17:10

Take constructive criticism to heart. Don't resent the criticism of others, since it presents an opportunity to grow as a human being. That doesn't mean that all criticism is right and should be used as a guidepost for living. But you should at least consider the possibility that improvements could be made, and strive to be and do your best.

Every set-back, every "NO!", every failure is a lesson for success. If you look for the reasons, the "why's," you'll quickly add wisdom for future decision-making. Experience is the road map to success.

*We admire the strength of youth
and respect the gray hair of age.*
Proverbs 20:29

When we are young, everything seems possible.
When we are older, we learn that limitations exist,
but there are still ways to achieve our goals. The
headstrong leaps of youth do not necessarily take us
further than the cautious stride of maturity.
Whatever your age, there is someone to learn from,
and something new to learn which may keep you
from making a mistake.

Take one day a week and spend some time with
someone older than you, in your job or in your
personal life. What you can learn through
friendships like this, with a relatively small
investment of time, can save you years of making
mistakes on your own.

Learning from your own experience

1. List three lessons you have learned the hard way.

2. Think of three people who have given you constructive criticism. Did you learn from them?

3. List experiences which taught you something as a child, as a young adult and very recently.

THE SEVENTH SECRET:

Helping others with acts of generosity and kindness will make you happy.

Be generous
and you will be prosperous.
Help others,
and you will be helped.
Proverbs 11:25

Generosity is more than giving to specific charities and dropping something in the collection plate. Having a generous nature includes helping those who need help in many ways, whether it is a kind word at a dark time, or a helping hand to a stranger. The person who cultivates this kind of generosity will succeed and become prosperous because he will be trusted.

You have been helped in your life by generous people, starting a chain of good that will go on and on. You pay back the kindness and generosity shown you by showing the same selfless giving and helping to others.

If you want to be happy,
be kind to the poor;
it is a sin to despise anyone.
Proverbs 14:21

Knowing we can help someone gives us a genuine feeling of joy. We can be the source of happiness to others, and in doing so, bring happiness to ourselves. When we fall for the short-term happiness of spending selfishly on ourselves, we short-change ourselves in the long run.

Those less fortunate than we are **need** our help. To despise them when they are in need is to invite others to despise us when **we** are in need. It's just a question of time. We all need help sometime.

Whenever you possibly can,
do good to those who need it.
Never tell your neighbor
to wait until tomorrow
if you can help him now.
Proverbs 3:27-28

The stresses of today's world place upon us a burden too heavy for some to bear. We need to be aware of those around us in need, by focusing **outward** more often than we focus **inward**.

Our generosity and assistance, no matter what form they take, can help relieve some of the burden and have a huge impact on someone else's outlook. We can each restore the hope that many people lose when they ask for help and don't receive it.

*You do yourself a favor
when you are kind.
If you are cruel,
you only hurt yourself.*
Proverbs 11:17

Kindness is something you can give away every day and something that everyone appreciates receiving. If you share nothing else, give of yourself through kindness. It may be a smile, a spoken word of encouragement, a helping hand to a stranger or a message of love to someone close to us. If you show kindness toward all, you show that you care about those around you.

There is too much cruelty in the world. Each of us feels the effects of that cruelty, but we have the power to overcome it, just by being kind every day, in every way we can. By adding to the cruelty, we wallow in the world's cruelty and hurt ourselves by shutting out the light of kindness.

Don't take advantage of the poor
just because you can;
don't take advantage
of those who stand helpless.
Proverbs 22:22

Never take advantage of others, but especially avoid taking advantage of those who rely upon you or who can't take care of themselves. No matter how just you may think you are in doing so, others will only see you as a bully or an opportunist.

When you find yourself in a weakened position, you don't want others to feel you deserve to be there. Protect the weak, aid the needy, and you will always have those who will come to your aid. It's just like the classic movie *It's a Wonderful Life*. Those who help others, especially those less fortunate, will never lack for friends and will be blessed.

Being kinder and more generous

1. Think of three people who have been kind or generous to you.

2. Make a list of three things you give to others on a regular basis or three ways you **could** help others.

3. Today, perform three "random acts" of kindness and generosity.

Order Form

I would like to order _____ copies of
Wisdom & Wealth
at **$12.95** each,
plus $2.00 for shipping and handling.

Please send me FREE information on other books to
help organize and simplify my life.

Send order to:
Solomon Press
c/o Don Jacobs
3205 South Meadow
Sioux Falls, SD 57106

Name_____

Address_____

City_____

State, Zip or Postal Code_____

Phone *(area code first)*_____

E-mail address_____

Thank you for your order.
We will ship your books immediately!

Order Form

I would like to order _____ copies of
Wisdom & Wealth
at **$12.95** each,
plus $2.00 for shipping and handling.

Please send me FREE information on other books to
help organize and simplify my life.

Send order to:
Solomon Press
c/o Don Jacobs
3205 South Meadow
Sioux Falls, SD 57106

Name_____

Address_____

City_____

State, Zip or Postal Code_____

Phone *(area code first)*_____

E-mail address_____

Thank you for your order.
We will ship your books immediately!